THE MEANING OF SEX
Walter Trobisch

BETTER IS YOUR LOVE THAN WINE
Jean Banyolak

answers are biblically and psychologically sound, understandable, and practical ... The thoughts, feelings, attitudes, words, actions, gentleness, encouragement, and special expressions of love are discussed in exceptionally good taste."

—**Dr. John Katter**
Former professor of Practical Theology and Pastoral Counseling, Springfield, Missouri. Assemblies of God Theological Seminary.

THE MEANING OF SEX

By Walter Trobisch

BETTER IS YOUR LOVE THAN WINE

By Jean Banyolak

Quiet Waters Publications
Bolivar, Missouri
2007

Quiet Waters Publications
P.O. Box 34, Bolivar, MO 65613
E-mail: QWP@usa.net
For other titles, prices, and order information:
www.quietwaterspub.com

Front cover design by Kevin Keller

ISBN 1-931475-29-6
[ISBN 9781931475297]
Library of Congress Control Number: 2005910830

CONTENTS

FOREWORD
BY INGRID TROBISCH

The night was Wednesday, September 19, 1979. The place was the Gross Chem Building at the University of North Carolina in Chapel Hill. Students—groups, couples, singles—streamed into the auditorium. They had seen the poster: WALTER TROBISCH, an internationally known author and counselor will lecture on *The Meaning of Sex*. And now they came, eagerly and full of curiosity.

The students could not know that for some of them this evening would be a life-changing experience. After listening intently to the message, they would await their turn throughout the night to speak to this man privately, not to argue or discuss, but to confess where they had disobeyed God's law. Walter Trobisch, who knew the power of forgiveness in his own life, would then place his hand on the head of each one who came and share with them God's promise of forgiveness.

None of us dreamed it would be his last lecture on earth. Walter and I, together with our third son Stephen, were on our way home from a missionary trip around the world. Three months earlier, as we had left our little home in the foothills of the Austrian Alps, I asked Walter what he was looking forward to the most on this extensive trip. "To the day when I can cross this threshold again and we are safely back home," he replied.

After we had spent a month in Indonesia, one of the missionaries there wrote to me:

> *Walter's ministry in Indonesia was like the last burst of sunlight—a last fulfillment of his calling. Two thousand Christians from the 800 islands of Indonesia had come together for a week to hear his message on love and marriage.*

Now we were safely home at the Lichtenberg. It was there on October 13th, 1979, that Walter, an early riser, came into our bedroom with a tea tray. We would drink a cup of tea, read the Daily Texts, share our thoughts and pray together. But this morning was different. As he opened the drapes and let the glorious October sun into our room, he said matter-of-factly, "Ingrid, my body is trying to tell me something and I don't understand it." A moment later, he took his last breath.

That was more than 25 years ago. Thanks to Dave and Sherry Hall, Mary Chiles, my sons David and

Stephen, this last message of Walter's has just recently been transcribed from a poor quality cassette tape to this printed form. I want to thank also our photographers David and Cathy Nehmer.

Author and counselor, Paula Rinehart, wrote after reading Walter's talk to the students at Chapel Hill:

> *I am so struck by the timelessness of it. ... There are so many seminal ideas here that others like myself have built on. I think God really used you both to open a door in the Body of Christ and to bring a legitimacy to a dialogue about sexuality that spoke of the freedom and the beauty that is uniquely possible to two people who know the whole story.*

THE MEANING OF SEX

A Lecture

By Walter Trobisch

One couple describes intercourse this way. I'm quoting from the book *Love is All: Conversations of a Husband and a Wife with God!* by Dr. and Mrs. Joseph Bird.

We made love last night,
    and today is new,
        brand new and alive. ...

We made love and everything was re-created. ...
    We talked,
        we laughed,
        and we prayed together with our bodies.

And You were so very present.
    It's then that You always are,
        especially then.

Our closeness to each other
    Increases and makes more alive
        Our closeness to You. ...

And this morning?
  This morning is sunrise,
    and growing things,
      and feelings of anticipation.

Today is new, brand new and alive,
  and the spiral of our love-making goes on,
    drawing us together upward,
      toward You.[1]

After a recent lecture, I talked with many of you. When I was sitting in the plane and reflecting on these thoughts—the suffering that was conveyed to me and the tears that were shed—I thought there must be a tremendous, deep misunderstanding or ignorance of what the sexual union is all about. This is why I have chosen the subject, "The Meaning of Sex."

When I talk about it, I talk about it as a Christian. When I talk about this subject as a Christian, I have to start with a confession of guilt—which we Christians have loaded upon ourselves because most of us have a broken relationship to the body. All of us, or most of us, still cling to the philosophy that goes back to Plato, which connects the things of the spirit with God. The material, the physical things, we connect with

---

[1] Joseph W. Bird and Lois F. Bird, *The Freedom of Sexual Love* (New York: Doubleday & Company, 1967)

something far away from God, if not sinful, at least dirty.

This becomes very clear, for instance, when I talk to parents, about teaching their children sex education. This is a worldwide difficulty for Christians. It is not cultural. When I talk in Africa about this, they say, "Mr. Trobisch, this is something Europeans or Americans do. To us in Africa, this is taboo. We cannot talk about sexual matters."

When I talk to American parents about these matters, they say, "Mr. Trobisch, you have lived too long in Africa. The Africans are closer to nature. They can do that."

And might I ask you a question? Which one of you is actually satisfied with the sex education you got from your parents? Would you like your children to have something better?

Platonic thinking, which suggests that the body is not of God, is entirely unbiblical. The Bible has the highest respect for the body. It begins with the body (the body was created before the soul) and it ends with the body (resurrection) when all of us will receive a new body. The Bible makes this statement in I Corinthians 6:19-20: "Do you not know that the body is a temple of the Holy Spirit, who is in you, whom you have received from God? You are not your own, you were bought at a price. Therefore honor God with your body." (NIV)

I know Christian couples who pray together every night before they go to sleep, except when they have intercourse. Then they don't pray. They have this feeling, "This is not really something which comes from God." Something is wrong here. Maybe you realized and noticed this in the poem by Joseph and Lois Bird: "praying together with our bodies!"

Intercourse is a form of prayer—a form of adoration of the Creator. Maybe much of this confusion in the world today rests with us, because we Christians have not talked about it. Who else can talk about it if not we Christians?

That is why I have chosen this subject, because I want to make good this sin of omission. I want to apologize to all those who have suffered because of our silence. Insofar as the Christian ethic is true, and insofar as it conforms to the will of God, it is true for all men, because God is the father of all men regardless of whether they recognize this or not. It does not make any difference to the truth. And the truth of creation speaks for itself.

Interestingly enough the Bible does not use this term *intercourse*. When the Bible speaks about this reality— the reality that human beings, male and female, come closest to each other—it uses another term, the term *one flesh*. *The two become one flesh.* This expression, *one flesh* is a very deep word that conveys in the Hebrew language, finality, irrevocability, durability, and utmost sincerity. It conveys commitment, complete commitment. It conveys communication, fidelity, but especially uniqueness. In order to convey this, the term *one flesh*—this reality of becoming one flesh is linked together intricately, interrelated with two other realities. This is best expressed in a short Bible verse, the only verse referring to marriage, which occurs four times in the Bible at very decisive places. It sums up the creation story. When Jesus is asked the question of divorce, he quotes this verse. In Ephesians, the Apostle Paul relates this verse directly to Jesus Christ. It says: "A man leaves father and mother; cleaves to his wife; and they become one flesh."

So this *one flesh* reality is inseparable from the two other realities described by these two simple words, *to leave* and *to cleave*. The leaving of father and mother—every word is important here—means that marriage is not a private or secret experience. It is related to society, to the family, represented first of all by father and mother. The family is part of society. Because it points outwardly, marriage is celebrated in all parts of the world with a public feast.

In Africa, for instance, the bridegroom picks up the bride at her home. Then the whole wedding party dances to his home. Sometimes three or four hundred people. Sometimes ten or fifteen miles from the village of the bride to the village of the groom. This is leaving. I understood for the first time in another culture what this leaving really means. These two are now husband and wife.

There is still a shadow of this public event here in American culture, for example, when you decorate the wedding car. Some still honk the horn while driving to the reception after the wedding ceremony.

This public act makes the marriage legal. The responsibility conveyed in the term *one flesh* demands legality. By the way, these words were prophetic words. They refer to equality. A man leaves father and mother. A man? Why not the woman? No. In a patriarchal society like Israel, it was a matter of course that the woman had to leave. But it was a revolutionary message—unpopular I'm sure—in Israel. The man, too, has to leave.

This verse protects the female rights in a patriarchal society. Both have to leave. Only in this leaving can the second reality come to pass—to cleave. Again, a very deep word. It means literally in Hebrew *to be glued together.* If you glue two pieces of paper together and then try to separate them, you tear both. They become inseparable. Divorce means that both are hurt, husband and wife, as well as the children. But the word cleaving conveys also that the two become closest to each other. Closer than to anyone else. Closer than to anything else.

I'm really happy that the Bible does not use the term *love* here but the term *cleaving.* Cleaving is love. It is a special kind of love, no longer a groping, and a *trying out* of love. It is love that has made a sober decision of will. I want to cleave to you for life. It is very difficult for me to give you the whole feeling behind these words. Therefore, I will often quote poetry and refer especially to the work of Ulrich Schaffer, a German-Canadian poet, who has in a very unique way, put into words the experience of his own marital life. The following poem is entitled: *The Work of Love.* This is very important if you want to understand this meaning of intercourse.

> *we have been told*
> *that love overwhelms us*
> *we have been shown in films*
> *that people fall in love in an instant*
>
> *we have read*
> *that yet others simply could not help themselves*
> *and had to become unfaithful to their partners*
> *we have heard the champions of free love declare*
> *that monogamy is unnatural*
> *we have been brainwashed to believe*
> *that love depends on our good looks*
> *and driving the right car*
> *we have been told*
> *that love comes*
> *and goes*

but very few have talked to us about
the work of love
about the energy expended to forgive
about the strain to survive the daily grind
with a heart still capable of loving
about the task of self-sacrifice
without dying in the process
about the use of the will
against the weakness of our emotions

the work of love
the energy to love
the decision to continue loving
in the hope of being transformed beyond ourselves[2]

In this leaving, the separation that has taken place can be compared to cutting the umbilical cord of this couple from their parents. This work of love cannot be done without a certain maturity and capability to withstand great tension. The poet Schaffer puts this in the following words:

I am closest to you
and you naturally hit out at me

---

[2] Ulrich Schaffer, *A Growing Love* (Harper & Row, Publishers, Inc. New York, 1977)

used me as your scapegoat
and I in my immaturity reacted
by hitting back
by blaming you
by making you my scapegoat
the difference was:
you were fighting for your life
while I was only reacting
you were fighting for your identity
while I was only fighting to maintain my honor
my sense of being right
I will now take it as a sign of love
when you lash out at me
when you kick to remain free
I know that you must trust me enough
to choose me as the person
through whom you want to grow[3]

You see, it is this growth process of love. Not falling in love, but this standing up in love, and this enduring pain, which is really significant if we want to start understanding, what the meaning of the sexual union is supposed to be. Growth, as I have said before, is always connected with pain. It is painful to grow through the three phases of love: the *auto-erotic* phase

---

[3] Ulrich Schaffer, *A Growing Love* (Harper & Row, Publishers, Inc. New York, 1977)

when the crush and the infatuation experiences come, the lover's feuds, the feelings of being rejected. This is a time of growth in handling masturbation by learning slowly not to change tension immediately into pleasure. Then comes the *homo-erotic* phase of love: being strong enough to relate for the first time to another person similar to me. This is a very important phase of the girl-girl and boy-boy friendships. It is only after this phase that a person becomes mature enough to enter the "otherliness" of the other sex, the *hetero-erotic stage*. Men and women are not the same. In one sense we will always be strangers to one another.

Attending one of our marriage retreats, a Danish colleague told his American brothers on Columbus Day that Columbus died without knowing he had discovered a continent. "Don't you men die without discovering your wife," he added.

The one who I cannot predict is the one of whom, in the final analysis, I am most afraid. Yet I am able to overcome my fear by reaching out to my wife and placing my confidence in her. I stand before her, naked and not shamed. I am completely myself. It is only when we have reached this maturity, that the reality of becoming one flesh can be experienced. It means, of course, much more than uniting two bodies.

The one flesh reality means to share, to share every-thing—not just my body—but also my heart, my thinking, my planning. I can share my joys, my wor-ries, and my fears. Even my guilt and failure. In doing this, I allow the other one to become completely her-self and accept her as she is. You see, many think marriage means that he is 50% and she is 50% and the two make 100%. But if two half-portions, Mr. 50% and Miss 50% get married, they often cancel each other out and are fortunate if added together they make 25%. We know that two halves never make a good marriage. It is only if we allow each other to be com-pletely herself and himself, 100% he and a 100% she, that the two make a new entity.

I have found this deepest mystery of marriage best conveyed in a very simple African wood carving be-low.

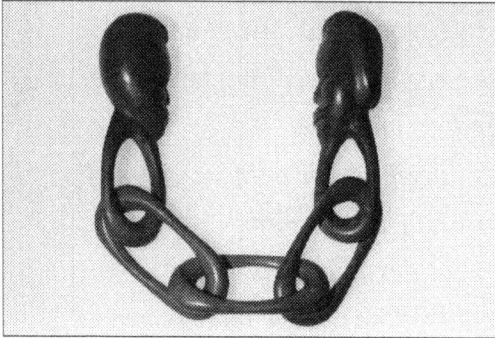

This is a marriage chain, a gift of the African church to every couple married in the church in order to re-mind them of their wedding vows. It is a carving of a woman and a man. After they have left, there are no strings attached. Now they are free to cleave. But the most beautiful thing is that if you could look closely you will see that there is no joint because the sculpture is carved out of one piece of wood. They are literally one flesh. They are one flesh, but remain two persons. The two have become one. Yet while they are one, they are still two. It is this mystery that has to be experienced. It cannot be understood intellectually. It has to be lived, and to live it, is the work of love.

Now to hit the same nail on the head a second time, may I share another poem by Ulrich Schaffer, entitled *As I Move Away From You*. Here he describes the 200% couple:

> *as I begin to be more self-sufficient*
> *as I become more independent of you*
> *as I begin not to "need" you*
> *as I begin to accept my loneliness*
> *and explore it*
> *as I begin to live without expectation of you*
> *as I refuse to live up*
> *to your expectations of me*
> *as I lose the need to react because*
> *I am finding my identity*
> *as I delve into my own depths*
> *unaccompanied by you*

and as you do the same

the miracle takes place:
you come closer
we learn from each other
we share
we fulfill expectations
we create a pull
because now the confines are gone
now we are no longer shackled to each other
we are no longer bound and tied by our "love"
we are free
we are in love
a renewed love
we are a gift to each other
unexpected and surprising
far beyond our hope[4]

The act of love is the physical expression of this marital sharing. It is only possible to become one flesh when related to these two realities of leaving and cleaving. You may be able to have sex outside of mar-

---

[4] Ulrich Schaffer, *A Growing Love* (Harper & Row, Publishers, Inc. New York, 1977)

riage, or before marriage, but you can never become one flesh.

I can best convey this interrelatedness of these three realities through this triangle.

Leaving

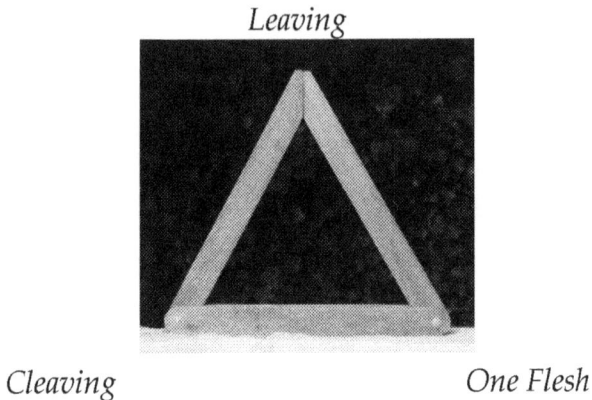

Cleaving   *One Flesh*

Here you see the leaving corner and the cleaving corner. There is no leaving without cleaving, and no cleaving without leaving. Only when this takes place, the reality of becoming one flesh becomes possible. Only as an expression of this one- flesh unity does the sexual union receive its meaning.

This is, I believe, our Christian message today in the confusion of this world: the message of the interrelatedness of these three realities. Today we tear this triangle apart; we separate marriage from love, and marriage from sex, as we see in adultery and in divorce. Or we separate love and sex as we see in prostitution.

In other words, in this life, the sexual act receives its highest dignity. It is unique, final, and irreversible. It is the most elementary form of self-giving and self-finding. It transforms two hitherto separate persons into a couple. Consequently these two beings surrender themselves to each other and enter into a mutual agreement, specific and unique, which remains a secret shared by them alone. In becoming one flesh, the couple partakes in an act whose implications cannot be reversed. Two human beings who have shared the sex act can no longer act toward one another as if they had not done so. The unity achieved from this "I—thou" experience transcends the biological dominion and reflects their shared participation in a profoundly significant experience. Once the two persons have had sexual intercourse with each other they can never again be in the same state as they were while they were virgins. The flesh has had an indelible stamp imprinted upon it. A person cannot divorce himself or herself from his or her own body.

Now you see why the Bible places so much emphasis on virginity. People say, "What does the Bible really say about premarital sex?" "Where is it forbidden?" This is implied in the high esteem of virginity, which means that often in a physical sense, especially for the young woman and in a lesser degree for the young man, they are physically, after their first sexual encounter, not any more the same. For instance, when

Isaac courted Rebecca, and the servant saw her for the first time, it says that "the girl was very beautiful, a virgin; no man had ever lain with her". (Genesis 24:16 NIV).

In order to emphasize this is not just a double standard, when they brought the adulteress to Jesus, he demanded the same purity from the man saying, "Let he who is without sin among you, be the first to throw a stone at her". (John 8:7)

Now you see this unique secret that only two persons can share—for a man to cleave to one wife—means that monogamy is not just a product of human culture. It is the inevitable consequence of a true love relationship. By putting sexuality and love to the test of durability and fidelity, marriage provides love with the proof of its authenticity. Marriage is necessary to love as a means by which it is purified and sanctified. This is the reason why I show this by a simple triangle.

When intercourse takes place and something less than this image is expressed, something less is the result. That is the reason for the suffering expressed in this poem taken from my wife's book, "The Joy of Being a Woman". Ancelle, a French woman describes her sexual experience:

… this body … tormented.

In the burning coals of our union, it is so seldom that
it reaches the goal—that it begins to vibrate!

Even though I desire it with all my heart
And want it with all my will
nothing happens.

It is like a motor which refuses to start—or it
Starts, and then turns over for a long time,
But without getting any place.

I hate myself. I'm beginning to fear these nights
Which do not really help us to find each other!

John seems to be satisfied. Is he really?

I hide from him the dissatisfaction which he
Does not know how to satisfy.

Joy—it is something meant only for the husband?
But of what use is joy that is not shared?
Tension mounts within me.
Toward what end? I do not know ... [5]

---

[5] Ancelle, *Mystère du Couple.* (Paris: Les Editions Ouvrières, 1967) p. 15.

When a married couple comes to me for counseling, and the husband says, "I'm too quick. I can never meet my wife's expectation and satisfy her fully." I always turn back the film, and what do I find? I find that they got used to having sex without conveying the reality of being one flesh in the deep meaning of the term. When that reality is not conveyed, it simply does not work. Especially through what you call petting (or making out) the young woman gets used to a very superficial sexual reaction that later on in marriage cannot be changed as quickly and simply as one might think. Also the young man, through this sort of mutual masturbation, gets used to a very quick release that later on hinders him from helping his wife to full satisfaction in marriage.

You see, the sexual experience of a woman is different than that of a man. Her curve of pleasure starts much slower, and then comes to a plateau of feeling where she can remain for a while before descending very slowly. A young man can be aroused very quickly, his feeling goes up steeply and after his ejaculation, his desire goes down to zero. It is imperative that a couple recognize this difference. It cannot be done in a superficial premarital relationship where there is often no feeling of shelter or of sincerity and no durability is conveyed. The man's ejaculation is not the same as the full and deep orgasmic experience of the woman.

What is confusing about the relationship is that when this act of intercourse has taken place without the meaning of being one flesh, the whole decision of getting married gets confused. This act, which conveys finality, has to be parallel with a decision of finality.

Allow me to share a letter I received from a young woman student here in the United States. She is a deep Christian, but she has had sexual relations with her boyfriend. This is what she writes:

> *I'm still struggling with what to do about Mark. I know that I need time away from him so that I may see the Lord's will for my life more clearly. My struggle is this; how am I going to tell him that I cannot see him for a while? I don't know how long it will take before I know whether or not I love him. The finality of the decision also frightens me. It seems I must decide right now whether or not I will marry. If I continue with our relationship, it will be the same as a yes, and if I don't, it will be no. I don't think there are any in-betweens. There are no gray areas. I don't feel prepared at this time to make such a decision and I don't want to hurt him but I know that things won't get any better if I don't make the decision now.*

You see the utter confusion of doing an act of finality and irrevocability and at the same time not being ready to make a final decision. In his poem *Caricatures of Marriage* Ulrich Schaffer describes what happen if a couple gets married on this basis:

> *Their marriage began with their bodies*
> *And never moved beyond them*
> *And now*
> *They indulge in legalized prostitution.*[6]

How many marriages are legalized prostitution because they started with the body and never moved beyond that? Now, in order to show you the difference of what intercourse could convey in the one flesh reality, I will read again from *The Joy of Being a Woman* the description of a marital experience:

> *... perhaps the word TOTAL would be more descriptive of the mature female orgasm. It is an orgasm, which starts deep within her body — subjectively, at least in the vagina — and extends, as it increases in intensity, to every part of her body, seemingly to the tips of her fingernails. At its peak, her whole being seems to dissolve and she*

---

[6] Ulrich Schaffer, *A Growing Love* (Harper & Row, Publishers, Inc. New York, 1977)

experiences an indescribable feeling of fulfillment and transcendence. She feels a loss of her ego boundaries as her entire being flows into him. It is an experience of such profoundness and meaning that no analogy is adequate to describe it, an experience which pervades and affects every aspect of her relationship with her husband, and one which makes the male orgasm seem almost rudimentary by comparison[7]

Now be honest and compare your experiences, make your own conclusions. It's always the same, when I talk to a young couple. Then I speak to the young woman alone and I ask her, "Was it really so wonderful?" Very often she starts to cry. She has experienced nothing. She was only afraid to lose her boyfriend. And he thought he had done her a favor.

Be honest with each other. Being honest is the first step of becoming one flesh. You will understand now why the Bible uses a special word to describe the reality of intercourse. It is the word "to know." Now to know in this biblical sense does not mean just to recognize each other intellectually. It means involvement, participation with that person in an experience which brings them to their true identity.

---

[7] Joseph W. Bird and Lois F. Bird, *The Freedom of Sexual Love* (New York: Doubleday & Company, 1967) pp. 170-171.

You must say to your mate: "To know you, I must make myself known to you. Disclose myself to the point of embarrassment. Allow you to see my confusion. To be naked and not ashamed. To share with you my journey which may appear so unattainable and so unrealistic. I must permit you to see me with clenched fists, with tears, in a daze of unbelief as well as beside myself with joy."

In full interaction and intertwining of our lives, we bring about new life, and carry in us the fruit of the union of body, mind, and spirit. This is the meaning of the sexual act. It is closely related to fertility.

"God created man in his own image, male and female he created them. And God blessed them and said to them, 'be fruitful and multiply'." (Genesis 1:28). Now in this age of contraceptive mentality, we tend to talk more about how to separate these two things, the sexual act and fertility. We have forgotten that originally and according to God's will they belong closely together. When we try to insert a technological short-cut, give the person a *thing* to solve the problem and think of all the ways we could prevent a pregnancy, it is very necessary to say to you the simple truth: *sex makes babies.*

I just came from Australia where engaged couples came to me for counseling. They wanted to get sterilized before marriage and asked me for advice. We live in a death-prone society. If we continue even with two-child families, we will die out. The tendency to interrupt the relationship between sexuality and fertility will always be at a disadvantage. There is no ideal solution—certainly not by using artificial means. But even if you use natural methods, and when you read my wife's book, you will see that we believe very much in natural family planning, even there you have disadvantages.

The normal thing is that the ones who have sexual intercourse also think of responsibility for a new life. There is no true marital love without the readiness to have children. The physical structure and the psychological complementarity of men and women were designed to equip them for parenthood. The whole biological process is oriented toward procreation. It determines the manner in which the sex organs function.

In the marriage liturgy of the Reformed Church of France, it says, "Grant them love and happiness to build a home in which Thy work of creation may be continued." When you have sex, you need to acknowledge the possibility of creating new life.

In order to demonstrate this connection and in order to let it sink in, I have often shown a film, made in France, where the camera was placed in the birthing room. It's like watching the Creator at work. It portrays the reality of the triangle of leaving, cleaving and becoming one flesh conveyed through the fact that this birth which should be the hour of the highest dignity of woman is experienced together as a couple. It is the mutual experience of husband and wife receiving their child together.

Jeremiah 1:5 says: "Before I formed you in the womb, I knew you. And before you were born I consecrated you." I read from Psalm 139:14-16:

> *I praise you because I am fearfully and wonderfully made; your works are wonderful, I know that full well. My frame was not hidden from you when I was made in the secret place. When I was woven together in the depths of the earth, your eyes saw my unformed body. All the days ordained for me were written in your book before one of them came to be.*

When Jesus died on the cross he prayed Psalm 22, the Psalm starts with "My God, my God, why have you forsaken me?" According to Jewish custom he prayed evidently the whole Psalm and here you will find the following words:

> *Yet you brought me out of the womb; you made me trust in you even at my mother's breast. From birth I was cast upon you; from my mother's womb you have been my God (vv. 9-10)*

Do you realize that Jesus—God himself—came to us through human birth by way of his mother's womb? Incarnation. Sex has to do with life. Can you understand your responsibility?

In the light of this one-flesh reality of bringing forth life itself, what do these words mean to you: abortion, homosexuality, pre-marital sex, intercourse, petting? What meaning do they convey?

My last word: our God gives everyone a chance for a new start. When I was an infantry soldier in World War II, after being wounded in Russia, I was put in the hospital. And I read my Bible. A man came to me and said, "There is no God. God is not almighty." I said, "How do you know?" He said, "One thing he cannot do. He cannot make done things, undone. He cannot cause things that have happened to u-happen." I was a young Christian at that time and I had no answer. But today I know from my own experience, that this is precisely what God can do. He can make happened things un-happen and done things undone—through forgiveness.

Let us pray:

> *Jesus,*
> *my friends and I live in a sex-oriented world. We are exposed to sex everywhere. Everywhere, your gift to us, the physical union as an act of love, is made cheap. In films and novels, in advertising and in the talking of people around us. Everywhere sex seems to be more important than love. And for many, love means just sex. Divorce from responsibility and from the decision to share life on a deep level—all that is left is "make love." And that kind of love is what you protested against, in one area of life or another. Few realize that that can never be love. We need you so desperately in this world if we want to experience our relationship as a gift from you, and if we are not to be washed away by the waves of cheapness. Help us, and teach us to wait, for your time, before joining our bodies.*
> *Amen.*

J. BANYOLAK

BETTER IS
YOUR *LOVE*
than wine

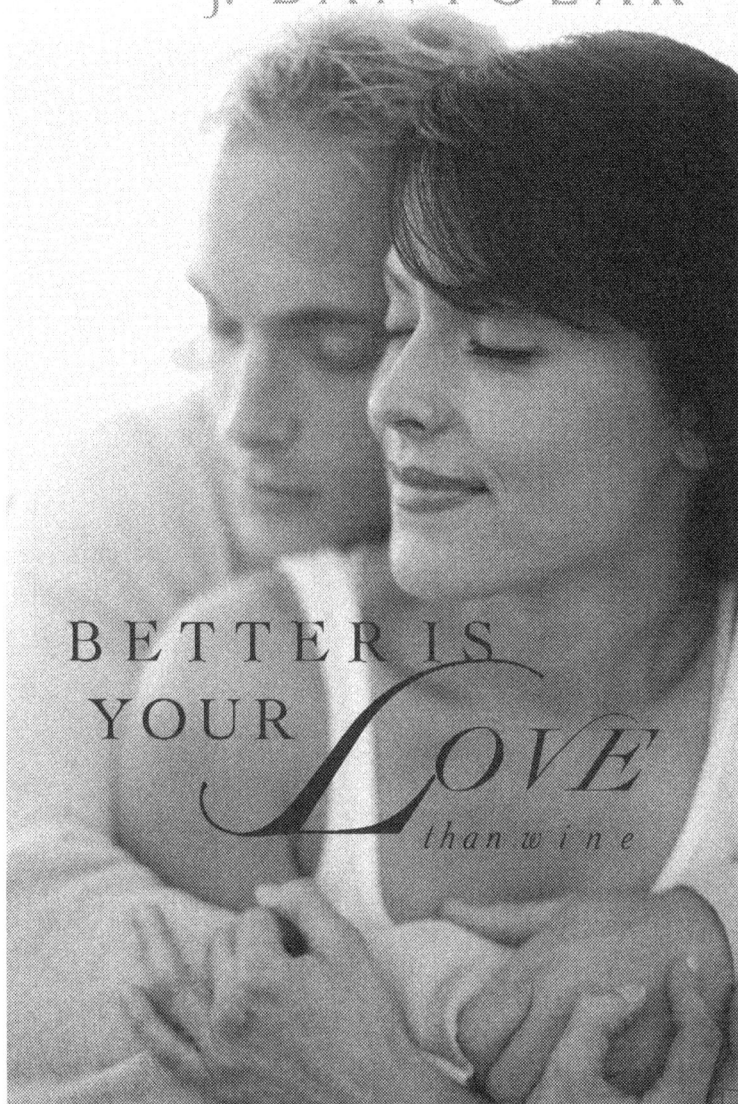

BETTER IS YOUR LOVE THAN WINE

By Jean Banyolak

CONTENTS

INTRODUCTION

Jean Banyolak is our colleague in family-life work in Africa. My wife and I greatly respect him for his instinctive wisdom, humility, and patience.

He was born in a small village in the virgin forest of Cameroon, West Africa, in 1942. After his graduation from Cameroon Christian College, he served as a teacher in Cameroon and then received training in marriage counseling in Europe. He and his vivacious wife Ernestine are the parents of two daughters and live in Douala, Cameroon, West Africa.

Two main factors determined the author's attitudes toward sexual matters from early childhood: one was the traditional African thinking; the other, a rather narrow religious upbringing. Both had this in common—sex is taboo, something which one does not talk about.

After having been exposed to sex education in a wider Christian context in Europe, Jean felt the necessity to interpret to his countrymen what he had learned. This was his motive in writing this book. While doing so, he was constantly fighting a two-front battle: on the one side against an African traditionalism for which talk about sex is close to sacrilege and on the other an unbiblical Christian conservatism for which sex is almost an equivalent to sin or at least something indecent which has nothing to do with the spiritual realm of life.

Jean stands up against both false concepts. He gives his fellow Africans, brought up in his traditions, the vocabulary which enables them to talk about sexual problems, while at the same time declaring that sex and God belong together.

The letters which Jean received from his African brothers and sisters speak for themselves. They give testimony of the great helplessness and ignorance, especially on the part of husbands. But they also indicate that sexual anticipation among African women is growing.

Those who read these letters attentively will soon realize that the problems they contain are certainly not limited to Africa. In spite of all the sex-saturated books, films and magazines, ignorance about basic sexual facts is still widespread even in Western cultures. The lack of understanding between the sexes is a universal problem as is the problem of unfulfilled sexual expectations.

Therefore I hope that this book, even though the author never dreamed of its publication outside of Africa, may be of help wherever it is read.

Walter Trobisch

AFRICANS WRITE ABOUT THEIR SEXUAL PROBLEMS

ABEL: "My wife has lost interest in sex. We were married two years ago. In the beginning, everything was fine. At times my wife even invited me. I saw and felt that she was really happy. She never resisted my approaches. Sometimes she even hurried to lock the door so that we could be alone. Both of us felt completely satisfied after the act. But now everything has changed. She doesn't invite me anymore. If I do, then her joy becomes sorrow. Sometimes she even gets nervous. She always sends me to lock the door and then she only gets half undressed. During the act, she makes faces. What shall I do?"

BENJAMIN: "Here's my problem. My wife has become cold. What are the cures for frigidity?"

COLBERT: "My wife no longer arrives at an orgasm with me. I am 38 years old and she is 24. I am told that she runs after young men of her own age. This troubles me a lot. Wouldn't it be wise for me to marry another woman?"

DANIEL: "My dear wife has started to lie to me. When I want to sleep with her, she sometimes tells me that she has her period or that she has a stomachache or a headache or her back hurts. When I bring her to the hospital for a checkup, each time the doctor says that she's in good health. When she goes to the market to buy food or the well to fetch water early in the morning, she sometimes deceives me. This is the moment when she goes to other men. The disturbance of our sexual harmony began three months ago. What can I do?"

EDWARD: "Should one talk or be silent during the sex act? I had an argument with my wife about this last night. My colleagues are not sure what to answer. Every one of us has a different opinion."

FREDERICK: "My spouse prefers to have the lights out during the act. Is this normal?"

WILLIAM: "As a close friend of yours, I am happy that you are now in Europe. How do they practice sex over there?"

ANNE: "I have a problem in my heart. I'm afraid to tell it to my husband, because I don't dare to criticize him. I find him rather brutal when we love each other in the evening. How shall I tell him this?"

BERTHA: "I just read the book called *I Loved a Girl*. I understand now that my husband ejaculates too early. How can this be treated? Can I help him to hold back?"

CHRISTINE: "My husband runs after college girls. He tells me that they learn how to make love at school. I answered him that I also shall learn from the college boys how to make love. He got very angry and would have beaten me if I had not run away. I wait for your advice about this."

ESTHER: "My husband demands that I yield to him every night. This is unbearable for me. When I tell him that this is too much he talks about marrying another woman. Tell me, how often is it normal for married couples to unite?"

FRANCES: "My husband never tells me beforehand when he wants to have intercourse. Sometimes, when I want to prepare the food, he calls me into the bedroom and undresses me. I'm afraid to criticize him, but this displeases me very much. Should a wife say no to her husband in this moment?"

GERTRUDE: "My husband goes to sleep very quickly after the sex act while I stay awake. He turns his back toward me and snores. This causes my satisfaction and joy to go away."

MARIE: "My husband is really the first man to whom I gave myself. But when we had intercourse for the first time we couldn't see any blood on the sheet. My husband reproaches me all the time that I wasn't a virgin, because he found my hymen already ruptured. What can I tell him to prove to him that I really was a virgin?"

AN OPENING WORD

It is certainly not easy to talk about sex. Why? Maybe because it is not customary to talk about sex. Many try to hide the fact that they have problems in this field and struggle along secretly. Nevertheless, these problems are burning ones for many couples and it is a pity that they are not able to express them. Even educated adults do not know the names of certain sex organs. Most of the parents of my country never talk to their children about sexual relations. As far as they are concerned, this realm is completely taboo.

The confidential letters which you have just read ask difficult questions and call for frank answers. Of course, in such a small book I cannot give complete answers, but I will be frank and mention briefly the way in which help can be found. These letters impel me not to be quiet on this subject which is so mysterious for many people. St. Clement of Alexandria has said, "It is not right that we are ashamed to call things by their names which God was not ashamed to create." Besides, the Bible speaks openly about sexual union in marriage.

I would like to emphasize that according to the Bible, physical union is an integral part of marriage. Genesis 2:24 says, "Therefore a man leaves his father and his mother and cleaves to his wife, and they become one flesh." This means that sexual relations before or outside of marriage do not correspond with the will of God. This has been explained in detail by Walter Trobisch in his book *I Loved a Girl*.

I have written this book for married couples. All the letters which I have quoted are written by married men or women and my answers therefore concern only married couples.

THE BIBLE SPEAKS
ABOUT SEXUAL LIFE

From the very beginning, God has given the gift of sexuality to man. Reproduction was one of the tasks God gave to the first couple in paradise. "So God created man in his own image, in the image of God he created him; male and female he created them. And God blessed them, and God said to them, 'Be fruitful and multiply, and fill the earth and subdue it ...'" (Gen. 1:27-28)

In Genesis 4 we read about the sexual union of the first human couple. "Now Adam knew Eve his wife, and she conceived and bore Cain ..." (Gen. 4:1)

In the middle of the Bible we find the Song of Solomon which is, in my opinion, the most beautiful of all love poems. Let me quote from the first chapter:

> *O that you would kiss me with the kisses of your*
> *mouth!*
> *For your love is better than wine,*
> *your anointing oils are fragrant,*

your name is oil poured out;
therefore the maidens love you.

(Song 1:2-3)

In the next chapter we find the description of a loving couple:

… refresh me with apples; for I am sick with love.
O that his left hand were under my head,
and that his right hand embraced me!

(Song 2:5-6)

The beauty and charm of a fiancée are described as more precious than all other earthly goods:

How sweet is your love, my sister, my bride!
how much better is your love than wine,
and the fragrance of your oils than any spice!
Your lips distil nectar, my bride;
honey and milk are under your tongue …

(Song 4:10-11)

The Bible does not despise the physical beauty of the human being:

How graceful are your feet in sandals,
O queenly maiden!
Your rounded thighs are like jewels,
the work of a master hand.

Your two breasts are like two fawns,
twins of a gazelle.
Your neck is like an ivory tower.
Your eyes are pools in Heshbon,
by the gate of Bathrabbim.
Your nose is like a tower of Lebanon,
overlooking Damascus.

(Song 7: 1.3-4)

A true lover wishes to have a secure place in the heart of the one whom he loves:

Set me as a seal upon your heart,
as a seal upon your arm;
for love is strong as death,
jealousy is cruel as the grave.
Its flashes are flashes of fire,
a most vehement flame.

(Song 8: 6)

The New Testament is not hostile to the human body either. Jesus himself was no enemy of the body. In the incarnation of God in Christ and through the resurrection of the body which we confess in our Creed, the human body is sanctified.

According to the New Testament, our bodies are a temple of God.

Do you not know that you are God's temple
and that God's Spirit dwells in you?

(1 Cor. 3:16)

The Bible does not despise the human body. Every Christian should be thankful to God for his body. A couple united in love should receive the pleasures sensed through their bodies as a precious gift from God. I appreciate very much the following statement from the book, *Amour et fiancailles,*[8] which means *Love and Engagement*:

"Sexuality is not the fruit of sin as some people claim. Before the fall of man, God had already created in him his sexual life. But this sexual life has been put out of balance by sin. Instead of leading man to fellowship and joy, it has often contributed to his destruction. If God has created sexuality and if Jesus has never declared that it is impure, there is absolutely no reason why it should cause in us feelings of shame."

Why not talk about it then?

---

[8] Editions Labor et Fides, Geneva.

SEXUAL UNION IN MARRIAGE

Sexual relations are not only physical or anatomical, but also psychological in nature. In other words, what is essential is connected much more with the thoughts and feelings toward one's self and one's partner than with the sex organs. The act of love is an intimate encounter of the whole male person with the whole female person. It is the total union of body, soul, and spirit. With these facts in mind, I answered the first letter quoted in this book, that of Abel who wrote: "My wife has lost interest in sex."

In the realm of love, there are no general rules applicable to everyone. Each couple has to find their own way. Nevertheless, certain elementary steps of the sex act are the same all over. This was a part of my answer to William who asked: "How do they practice sex in Europe?"

The act of love consists of three different stages: preparation for intercourse or love play, the sex act and the period of relaxation.

PREPARATION FOR INTERCOURSE OR LOVE PLAY

The period of preparation varies in length depending upon whether a couple feels the desire to unite as is their habit or whether they come together after a period of abstinence. There is also the possibility of a loving surprise. It can happen that the sexual desires spring up suddenly in one of the partners, that one transfers it to the other, and that both of them end up by wishing to unite immediately. In the case of such a loving surprise, the preparation can be shortened considerably.

Normally, however, the preparation should be much longer. If a couple plans to unite in the evening, their preparation could begin as early as in the morning. This long-range preparation is important for both husband and wife—but especially for the wife. The love of the husband for his wife is like a warm coat in which she is enclosed and sheltered. When she feels secure in this love at all times she can give herself to him and fully respond in the act of love. But if the husband is unkind or insensitive to his wife in the morning, then it is as if the coat is full of holes. He must not be astonished if in the evening she is not ready to respond to his approaches when he wants to unite with her. The wife must try to understand and be sensitive to her husband. The male ego is fragile. If the wife understands this, then she will not scold, mock, or condemn her husband in any area of life, especially in things pertaining to sexual love. Instead she will be appreciative of his care for her. To prepare for the act of love both the husband and wife must know what the partner needs and desires. If either is full of fear, unresolved conflict, or feelings of hurt or inadequacy, then he or she will draw back and not find the joy that is rightfully theirs in the act of love. The secret then is to be able to talk to each other and to share what hurts. To keep silent is harmful to both. In answering Frances' letter, I encouraged her to tell her husband frankly, with love and without being afraid, what she thinks about their sexual union. Of course, she should not do it at an inconvenient moment.

The question which Abel poses is different. He complains that his wife no longer invites him to have intercourse. Contrary to what most women think, it is not always the task of the husband to initiate physical union. The tender request of the wife may augment the desire of the husband and make him very grateful to her. If the partner does not voluntarily accept this loving invitation, it is preferable to wait rather than try to convince him or her to consent immediately.

The act of love is impossible without voluntary agreement. The location of the vagina proves that. It is not located behind as with some animals. It is between the legs of the woman, and the legs are the strongest parts of the human body. Any penetration, therefore, is impossible unless she opens her thighs voluntarily. If the sexual union with one's partner is to be successful, it is important to know beforehand that she fully agrees. If this is not the case, then the husband must continue to court her until she is willing to yield. Instead of doubling the power to force the other one to receive him, it is much better to double the courtesies, until the other one consents of his own will. In a gallant manner, the one who has the desire invites the other one. Then the two will agree about the proper time and place. Finally, they will give each other a kiss of expectation and promise.

From then on, the partners try to create an atmosphere of love. Each one aims at being well received in the other one's soul. They can succeed in this by doing as many things as possible together—going for a walk, listening to music, dancing as a couple, helping one another and exchanging views and comments. The lovers seek to express their sentiment in tender words. They play together, work together, even read together something of common interest.

Often being out in the open, breathing fresh air, will invigorate and animate them. Some couples like to surprise each other with gifts or small tokens of their love. In any case, it is essential that a feeling of joy be awakened in the partner. The role that physical cleanliness plays during the act should not be neglected. Christine complains in her letter: "My husband runs after college girls." I suggested to her that perhaps one of the reasons her husband is attracted to college girls is because they are always clean. College girls have learned about hygiene in school. Some couples make it a habit to take a bath or a shower as a preparation for their sexual union. A bad odor can extinguish erotic feelings, just as the smell of a certain perfume can awaken them. Therefore, it is well to conform to our partner's tastes. One must also be careful about bad breath. Women are sensitive to the smell of onions, alcoholic drinks, tobacco, or anything that is spoiled. Are we also ready inwardly to receive our partner and to give ourselves to him completely?

The place where the lovers unite should give them a feeling of security. Both of them, but especially the wife, can be very much disturbed by walls which are too thin, by doors which cannot be locked, by beds which are too narrow, too short or too noisy, by rooms too hot or too cold. It goes without saying that children should not sleep in the bedroom of their parents or else this will be a cause of disturbance, especially for the wife.

The moment approaches. Is everything ready and care taken that no killjoy knocks at the door? Nothing should bother or trouble this great moment of pleasure. The love play is now ready to begin.

A man desires to take and possess his wife, while her greatest desire is to surrender and be possessed. Here everything depends upon the skill of the husband. It is up to him to master the delicate art of winning over the heart of his companion; to prepare her by making her erotic desire grow and blossom. The main task of the wife in this moment is simply to relax and to be pleased by being pleased.

The most common mistake is for this time of preparation to be too short. This is probably the case with Benjamin whose wife has become frigid. Half an hour of preparation is the absolute minimum. The longer it takes, the more grateful will be the wife. Even a whole hour would not be too much or too long for her.

Generally, one can say that the time of preparation can never be too long. It can only be too short.

Here, I would like to repeat again that there are no rules or prescriptions which apply to every couple. The sexual union is a response born out of tender feelings and sensitive reflexes that should be completely spontaneous.

As to the question of undressing, Abel seems to be perturbed that his wife does not get completely undressed. Certain wives enjoy very much being undressed by their husbands. In this case, the husband does it gently and calmly, piece by piece. According to the lovers' tastes, the wife can be undressed completely or partially. Some couples prefer that the wife wear a very thin negligee or a soft, velvety nightgown.

As far as the man is concerned, he can undress himself or be undressed by his wife if she enjoys doing it. Some wives like their husbands completely naked; others prefer that the husband keep on his shorts until the moment of full union. It all depends upon the taste of the wife.

It is very important that after undressing the couple not be interrupted until after the period of relaxation. Otherwise, it is psychologically very troublesome.

Before the complete coming-together, the two exchange mutual gestures of tenderness which lead them gradually to a high sexual tension. This tension should then be satisfied and quieted by the union of love.

In order to carry one's partner to the height of sexual excitement, one has to know the erogenous zones, the parts of the human body most sensitive to erotic feeling. "To know" one's wife or one's husband means to know where these zones are.

If one is in good health, practically the whole human body reacts to erotic stimulation as a result of practice and certain psychological factors. Generally speaking, these erotic zones are located in the vicinity of the sex organs and around the orifices by which the interior of our organism communicates with the outside world. These are the lips, the mouth with all its parts including the tongue, the ear lobe, and the pavilion behind the ear. In addition, the armpits, the inside of the thighs and the area around the sex organs are also erotically sensitive.

The erogenous zones for the woman are especially the nipples and the area surrounding them on the breasts, the clitoris, the large and small lips which protect the vaginal opening, as well as the muscles at the interior of the vagina.

Some African tribes practice circumcision for the female as well as the male. By this operation the clitoris of the woman is cut out or severely damaged. One of the motives for this operation, called clitoridectomy, is to prevent the woman from having an orgasm or even any sexual pleasure. My talks with African, American, and European doctors lead me to discourage this operation. Sexual enjoyment in orgasm is God's gift to both husband and wife. In 1 Tim. 6:17, God has promised to give his children richly all things to enjoy. Through love, patience and practice it is possible also for the wife to know this joy.

The married couple embraces, exchanging caresses and kisses. All these gestures have but one goal—to excite the lovers sufficiently so that they are able to unite completely and easily.

What is the final stage of sexual excitement? The end of the male organ itself is completely rigid. The breasts of the wife swell and the nipples are erect. Her clitoris, at the upper end of the vaginal region, increases in size. Due to the increased blood supply in the vaginal region, a result of the gentle love play of her husband, the vagina becomes warmer and more moist, making it ready to receive the penis. The wife's breathing becomes more rapid and it is her ardent desire that the act may begin. In case the husband feels that his ejaculation is very close, then the couple should wait for a few moments before the second stage of the conjugal act begins.

THE SEX ACT PROPER

This is the decisive phase, the act of love itself. For its beginning, one condition must be fulfilled: The vagina must be moist. As just explained, this takes place when sensations from the clitoris cause little glands in the vagina to send out a fluid which lubricates the vagina and thus makes the entrance of the penis easier. If this has not taken place, sexual union will be painful for the wife and perhaps even displeasing for the man. Without this lubrication in the vagina there is even a possibility that small wounds may result. If you recall the letters quoted at the beginning of this book, I believe that Benjamin, Daniel and the husbands of Anne and Frances should ask themselves whether an inadequate preparation is one of the causes of their problems.

The couple may use any position they wish. The most common position is the one where the wife is lying on her back with her legs spread apart and a little bent. The husband is above her and supports himself by his elbows and knees in order not to bother her by his weight.

A position in which the woman is above is also poss-ible. Each couple should use the position which brings them the most joy and satisfaction. In fact, it is often advisable to change positions.

The penis can be guided in the beginning by the husband, but later more safely by the wife. It must be remembered that the vaginal conduct runs first up and then backward, and it is in this direction that the man tries to enter. A small membrane called the hy-men partially closes the entrance of a virgin. Carefully the husband breaks it and often, with this penetration, causes his young wife some pain and a little bleeding. In case the hymen persists after several attempts to break it (a rare condition), it is advisable to consult a medical doctor who will cut it easily.

I now come to the letter written by Marie, who says that her husband reproaches her that she was not a virgin because he found her hymen already ruptured. It is not just the existence of the hymen which charac-terizes the virginity of a woman. Often the hymen is ruptured by itself by a sudden movement of the legs, by the use of tampons during menstruation, or even by age. Virginity is above all the untouched reservoir of the ability to love.

After uniting, the lovers move together rhythmically and slowly. The husband may prefer to use up and down movements where the penis glides back and forth within the vagina, or round movements which go more from right to left, while the wife responds by movements of her own. Sometimes the wife has the most joy when she rotates in the opposite direction to that of her husband. The partners try to prolong these pleasant movements together as long as they are capable. It is desirable to make them last as long as possible, because the feeling of pleasure which the wife experiences rises more slowly than that of her husband. But aside from this fact, it is also true that this mutual exchange of happiness has a great meaning in itself for the fulfillment of marriage. Every rough movement is to be discouraged. Anne mentions in her letter that her husband is brutal. This can only lead to hurt feelings; it is destructive for any marriage.

Bertha states in her letter that her husband ejaculates too soon. In this case I would give him the following advice. He should ask his wife not to caress his penis any more after it has reached the state of erection. He may even try, slowly and gently, to enter her vagina before his organ has reached the complete stage of erection, for the entrance itself is a strong means of excitement. Immediately after entrance, the couple may pause for a short time so that the first wave of excitement will pass. It is also advisable that the man should not enter too deeply in the vagina, for the deeper he enters, the more contact he has, and the more intense is the stimulation. Also the wife experience her greatest sexual stimulation at a point only about 2-1/2 inches inside the vagina. Therefore it is important that the husband avoid too strong and too fast movements back and forth which only mask the sensations of his wife as well as cause him to have his ejaculation too soon. He should move very slowly with gentle pressure sideways toward the walls of the vagina. Filling the lungs with a deep breath and tightening the abdominal muscles has also proved helpful.

Psychologically it is sometimes helpful for the man to imagine that he is in the process of sucking something out rather than pouring something into. He should also try to concentrate his thoughts on non-erotic objects.

How should the wife behave in such a case? In answer to this question, one wife has given this confidential advice: "While my husband refrains his erotic feeling in order not to ejaculate too soon, I try to intensify my feelings. I am thankful to my husband that he makes an effort on my behalf in order that I also may reach the orgasm. This kindness and love on his part, this desire to help me, makes me very happy. By not just resting quietly, but by tenderly responding to his movements, I consciously yield to him my whole heart, my whole body, and all that I am as a feminine being. In this precious moment, I try to do only one thing: to relax and to let myself go completely. The more I get used to my husband, the more I am able to anticipate how close or how far away he is from ejaculation. If I am already highly stimulated and know that my orgasm is very close, while his is farther away, then I stimulate him by his favorite caresses in order that he may let himself go. But if I feel that he is already very close to the climax while I am farther away from it, I try to concentrate my whole thinking on erotic sentiments." This is the procedure by which you can try to experience the climax of sexual pleasure with your partner. It is this information which I shared with Colbert in answer to his letter.

By more vigorous movements, the husband leads his wife to experience an orgasm and ejaculates his sperm within the vagina. This seminal emission marks the masculine orgasm (Fig. a). The feminine orgasm is more difficult to determine (Fig. b). It can be recognized by the trembling of the wife's whole body as well as by rhythmical contractions of the vagina and uterus combined with a sucking-in motion, but above all by an insurmountable feeling of happiness and well-being, sometimes even by a temporary loss of consciousness.

To harmonize the sexual union means to endeavor to reach the orgasm at the same time as one's partner (Fig. d). Some husbands who reach the orgasm before their wife does, continue nevertheless with their movements and with caressing the erogenous zones until she also arrives at an orgasm. Other husbands disengage their penis and by gently touching the clitoris of the wife help her in this way to have an orgasm. However, this latter experience is not as satisfactory for both partners as the above-described one.

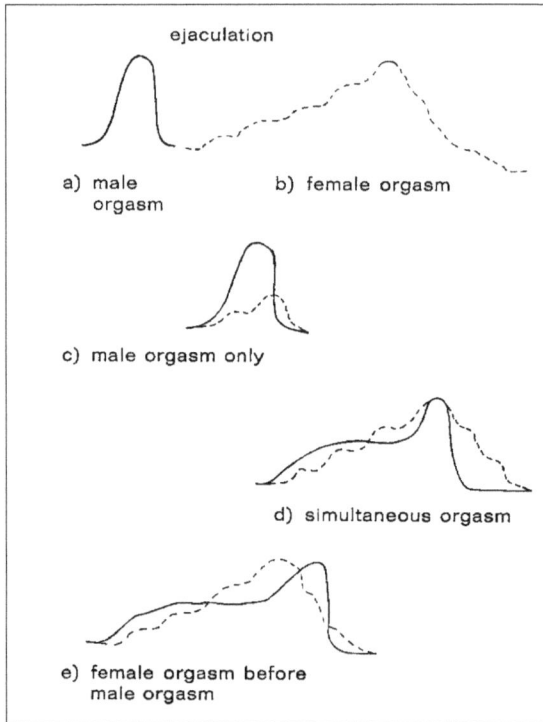

To harmonize the conjugal act is a desired goal, but marital happiness does not depend upon its achievement. There are many happily married couples who have never achieved it. And certainly it is not something that can be reached in a day. Therefore couples should not be discouraged if they have not found complete fulfillment in the act of love during the first months or even the first years of their marriage. Marriage is not a destination, but a journey. As a husband and wife make this journey together, growing and maturing and learning how to love, they will reach sexual harmony as a fruit of their good marriage. The problem which Benjamin writes about in his letter leads me to say a few words about frigidity. A woman is called frigid when she is incapable of experiencing sexual pleasure. Sometimes a woman is only partially frigid, as for example, when she has sexual desire but the sexual union is repugnant to her, or when she is able to have sexual pleasure during the sex act, but is incapable of reaching an orgasm or the relaxation which follows. In extreme cases of frigidity, the vagina is drawn together so that any penetration becomes impossible. This is called vaginism.

The causes of frigidity are, now quite well known. Only seldom is frigidity due to a physical deficiency, such as glandular troubles, general exhaustion or insufficient development of the organs. More often frigidity is psychological. In such cases it is often caused by a narrow and negative sex education, which pictures sexuality as something forbidden or indecent and in turn leads to a strong inhibition in the unconscious mind of the girl. Guilt feelings which go back to childhood and which may be caused by sex fantasies or masturbation can also be the cause of frigidity. Even an attachment too close to a girl's father, brothers, teacher, or former sweetheart can cause frigidity. Sometimes it is caused by a tendency to homosexual behavior or simply the fear of everything masculine and the refusal to accept the feminine role.

The danger of becoming frigid is naturally much greater for a woman who has undergone female circumcision. Frigidity is even the motive for this cruel operation because one defends it by saying: "Circumcised women are more faithful." And the reason given is that they are thus deprived of sexual pleasure. Nevertheless, although clitoridectomized women may not be able to have a clitoral orgasm, they can reach a vaginal orgasm. Learning how to do a very simple exercise can be of great help to these women. (Some doctors estimate that two-thirds of all women need help here and yet very few wives have ever heard of this training.)

Dr. Paul Popenoe of the American Institute of Family Relations reports that in a series of over a thousand cases of sexually unsatisfied women who asked for help, some 65 percent gained relief simply by doing this exercise. (Among the other 35 percent were those who had deep-rooted emotional problems as well as some cases of serious physical disease.)

Approximately 1-1/2 to 2 inches inside the entrance of the vagina is a band of muscle known as the pubococcygeus or Kegel muscle (named after Dr. Arnold Kegel of Los Angeles). The greatest source of sexual sensation has been found to be just beyond the upper edge of this muscle. This is particularly felt when the muscle is contracted or otherwise stimulated. Many women lack full sexual response because this upper portion of the muscle is not well developed.

Dr. Popenoe gives the following suggestions for training this muscle: "The Kegel muscle can be strengthened by 'pulling up' on it as if making a strong effort to shut off or hold back the flow of urine. A wife who lacks satisfactory sensation in the vagina or who is unable to have orgasm, should practice this regularly, keeping her feet spread a little apart. She may do so for a few minutes at a time, half a dozen times a day, even when she is engaged in some of her housework. Or she may count the contractions and plan on, say 300 a day, divided into groups of 50 each. Strengthening the muscles in this way usually narrows and lengthens the vagina and pulls the organs of the pelvis up into their proper position."

"It is a rare woman," says Dr. Popenoe, "who cannot heighten her sexual adequacy through this understanding and technique, by bringing these muscles surrounding the vagina into play during intercourse. We believe that this is a key to good sexual adjustment."

Sometimes the frigidity of a wife can be caused or aggravated by mistakes of the husband. Repeated awkwardness during the sex act, premature ejaculation, forcing the wife to yield instead of asking her to consent voluntarily, considering her as an object to satisfy his own desire, bad choice of time and place for the sexual union so that the wife feels insecure—all these mistakes on the part of the husband can lead his wife to frigidity.

Premarital sex is often practiced in situations which do not offer any feeling of security to the lovers. These relations are often accompanied by the fear of conception. Therefore these practices before marriage can actually be one of the causes of frigidity later on in marriage.

I explained these facts about frigidity when answering the letters of Abel, whose wife has lost interest in sex; of Benjamin, whose wife is probably frigid; and of Daniel, whose wife complains about backaches when the moment of sexual union approaches. In the case of frigidity, the couple tries to find out the causes or still better seeks the advice of a marriage counselor or medical doctor who can study the case and offer effective help. In his letter, Frederick wants to know whether it is normal to turn off all the lights during the sex act. This depends upon the couple. Some women cannot arrive at an orgasm unless the sexual union takes place in complete obscurity. For this reason, they always close their eyes during the act. These wives prefer the night when all the lights are out. Other couples prefer a very dim light and still others red or blue. Edward asks in his letter: "Should one speak or keep silent during the sex act?" Again there are no fixed rules. However, I would advise the couple to talk. God has given to human beings the gift of speech which animals do not have. It pays to ask our partner how he or she feels—to express in words what we would like for him or her to do and how we feel about it. It is certainly permitted and even recommended to make complaints and suggestions known to one's partner. This is what I advised Anne to do—to tell her husband frankly if she feels that he is brutal to her. Of course, one must choose the right moment. One should not talk about hurts on the spur of the moment, but rather choose a quiet place when there is enough time to listen to each other patiently. The one who is not able to listen to the partner's criticism does not really love. We now come to the last stage of the sexual union.

THE PERIOD OF RELAXATION

Following orgasm, the husband will have a feeling of satiation and even exhaustion. He desires sleep for he has used up his physical strength. Just as it takes the wife longer to reach the sexual climax and just as she approaches it in a more gradual manner, so it is with her after orgasm. It is as if she has reached the top of the mountain, and on the summit she has found a plateau, a tableland. She likes to stay there as long as possible and is reluctant to descend. Her great need at this time is to be held by her husband, to feel his support and strength and to be reassured through words and caresses of his love for her. If he withdraws from her embrace, turns his back to her and falls asleep immediately, maybe even snoring, then the marvel— the wonder of this moment—is broken. It is as if a light goes out and the wife has a feeling of emptiness and quiet disappointment. She may even feel abandoned.

Consequently a hostile feeling may arise in her. Her husband may appear to her as a thief who comes to steal her body and heart and who then runs off. But she must also understand her husband's tiredness.

After the orgasm, the partners feel moved to the depths of their being. Often they feel exhausted and sigh deeply. After the storm of passion the two lovers are intimately opened up to each other and can look straight into each other's souls. They can now say and reveal to each other things which would not otherwise find expression.

I have counseled the husband of Gertrude to make use of this moment of unity to talk intimately to his wife. After the orgasm, the partners continue to caress, to admire, to kiss each other and to express their mutual thanks before they separate their bodies from one another. They are especially thankful to God who is the creator of their partner and of the joy which they have just experienced. Often younger couples again feel excited after a while and wish to repeat the sex act. The partners then continue their love play or even sleep a little, resting in each other's arms. When they unite again, it is easier for the husband to prolong the act of love and then too the wife will usually reach her orgasm more quickly than before.

In marriage one may unite as often as desired. No one can make fixed rules in this respect. Neither should it become a routine—a scheduled program which is planned in advance. Otherwise we risk making the love act monotonous. This monotony is often the beginning of dissatisfaction.

The frequency of the conjugal act varies according to age, health and temperament of the couple. I would advise not to unite unless there is a real desire to do so. The partner who has the greater desire should adjust to the one who is less ardent and not the other way around. In any case, excess should be discouraged. Better two times not at all, than one time too many. Some couples like to unite twice a week, others three times. It may also happen that a mutual passion make them unite everyday. But then there may come a time when they wish to abstain for a whole week, or even two. It all depends upon what serves the conjugal peace best.

I cannot close this chapter without speaking about sexual self-control within marriage. Even married people cannot have intercourse at any time they might wish. Sickness, temporary separation while one partner is on a trip and pregnancy are some of the factors which impose sexual restraint also on a married couple. If one of them is sick and suffers, then he or she must concentrate all powers to fight pain and sometimes even the fear of death. In case of temporary separation, each partner lives in chastity in order to keep the conjugal fidelity which he and she have promised before God.

During pregnancy, abstention from sexual union is recommended during the last four to six weeks before the expected date of birth. Also after the wife has given birth, it is well for the couple to abstain from intimate relations for at least six weeks, when the wife's organs have returned to their normal state. As you can see, sexual self-control is necessary if a marriage is to be successful. This self-control is not easy to learn and therefore one must begin before marriage. The one who has not learned how to master his passions before marriage will have difficulty mastering them after marriage. Therefore the happiness of his marriage is at stake. The one who neglects to learn sexual self-control is heading blindly for failure. Good will and human strength alone are not sufficient to learn this self-discipline.

From all that I have said thus far, you may have the impression that all that counts for a successful sexual union is human wisdom and intelligence or simply following good advice in order to reach the goal. If you try this, you will soon experience defeat. Human power alone is not enough for a successful marriage. We would be lost if God himself were not willing to give us his power in order to put this counsel into practice. In order to be able to understand each other and to love each other intimately in the way I have described, it is necessary for each one of us to have a personal relationship with God.

Many couples, when they experience a crisis, forget completely the help and the power of prayer. I know couples who pray together every evening except when they want to unite sexually. They have the impression that the sex act and prayer do not fit together. This means they have separated their sexual life from their spiritual life. They consider the sexual union in marriage often as something dirty or even sinful and have a bad conscience about it. This is a great mistake. It is entirely unbiblical. God is the Lord *of* all realms of life, and this means also the sexual realm.

God wants to be close to us in whatever we experience and this is true also about the act of love.

AFTERWORD

This frank and enlightening book was originally published in French by our African co-worker, Jean Banyolak under the title *My Wife Has Lost Interest in Sex*. After receiving many letters from men who asked his advice, Jean decided it would be helpful to publish these letters for a wider audience. It was then that I translated the book into English to be published under the title of *Better is Your Love Than Wine* by InterVarsity Press, Downers Grove where it went through several printings.

The message of Jean's book is about the importance of taking time for the act of love. Charlie Shedd once said, "Sex is a twenty-year warm-up." If this is true, then we want to hear what Jean has to say.

Jean Banyolak died after a lingering illness on Good Friday, 2004 in Douala, Cameroon.

Ingrid Trobisch

Quiet Waters Publications
P.O. Box 34, Bolivar MO 65613-0034
http://www.quietwaterspub.com
Email: QWP@usa.net

I Loved A Girl

By Walter Trobisch
'Last Friday, I loved a girl—or as you would put it, I committed adultery.' This deeply moving story of a young African couple is Walter Trobisch's first book. It has become a classic with its frank answers to frank questions about sex and love. Its tremendous world-wide success led Walter and Ingrid Trobisch to leave their missionary post in Cameroon and start an international ministry called Family Life Mission.
ISBN 1-931475-01-6

I Married You

By Walter Trobisch
Set in a large African city, this story covers only four days in the life of Walter and Ingrid Trobisch. Nothing in this book is fiction. All the stories have really happened. The people involved are still living today. The direct, sensitive, and compassionate narrative presents Christian marriage as a dynamic triangle.
ISBN 0-9663966-6-9

Love Is a Feeling to Be Learned

By Walter Trobisch.   ISBN 1-931475-06-7